BRITNEY
SPEARS

First published in 1999 by
Virgin Books
An imprint of
Virgin Publishing Ltd
Thames Wharf Studios
Rainville Road
London
W6 9HT

A catalogue record for the book is available from the British Library.

ISBN 0-7535-0364-6

Designed by **nim** Design, London

Colour Origination by Colourwise Ltd, W Sussex

Printed and bound by Butler & Tanner Ltd. Frome and London

Picture Credits

BRITNEY SPEARS

THE UNOFFICIAL BOOK

MOLLY MACDERMOT

Contents

Dreams Can Come True

Some people recognize their passion early in life and use it to propel themselves to great heights of stardom. Britney Jean Spears is one of those people. She discovered at an early age that music was her passion and that, if she had her way, she was going to sing and dance her heart out for the rest of her life.

One of the first examples of Britney's drive to entertain came when she was five years old, singing "What Child Is This" in front of an amazed audience at her kindergarten graduation. Even then, before she had learned how to write her own name, Britney knew she loved performing in front of an audience. This brown-eyed girl from America's Deep South recalls her childhood love for music, when she would blast Michael Jackson's *Thriller* in the house and sing along repeatedly until she had practically worn out the tape – as well as her mother's patience. The voice that filled the Spears' home day after day would eventually fill the homes of millions of people around the world.

It was on January 19, 1999, exactly a week after the US release of her debut album *...Baby One More Time*, that Britney discovered her dreams of stardom had finally come true. She received a phone call that would literally wake her up to the fact that she was a huge success in the tumultuous world of music. The call came from her lawyer and the president of her record company, Jive, who wanted to personally deliver the phenomenal news that Britney's single "...Baby One More Time", and the album of the same name, had both scaled the Billboard charts to the number one position.

The voice that filled the Spears' home day after day would eventually fill the homes of millions of people around the world

Not only was her music a smash, but she was also the first female artist (and the youngest) to simultaneously land the number one single and number one album in the US. Through hard work and dedication she had achieved the unimaginable. Not bad for a girl who had just turned 17 the month before.

Britney would forgo sleep that memorable night to call her friends and family with the exciting news that she was number one

Britney was officially the fresh new face of pop, the hottest female teen solo artist in a music world dominated by an onslaught of boy bands. What that memorable phone call would really mean in Britney's heart was that millions of people were listening to her music and loving it. Now when Britney turned on the radio it was her very own voice filling the airwaves.

The album would fly off record store shelves around the world and reach triple-platinum status in the US within a few months of its release, a remarkable feat for a solo artist making her debut. Britney would forgo sleep that memorable night to call her friends and family with the exciting news that she was number one.

This was just the beginning for Britney. Not only was her album a permanent feature of the Billboard charts, but her sassy video for "...Baby One More Time" was gaining heavy rotation on MTV's popular music show *Total Request Live*. The video featured a carefree Britney dancing and singing through a school, sporting a micro mini and bare midriff – an outfit condemned by some critics as scandalous.

On top of the massive success of Britney's album and video, top designer Tommy Hilfiger asked her to be the new "Tommy Girl" and appear in his spring ad campaign. Britney's album was also making waves in the rest of the world. In the UK, the single's February debut had broken records by selling more copies in its first week of release than any debut single ever, even surpassing the first-week sales of the Spice Girls' Christmas hit "Goodbye."

Britney was suddenly everywhere, flooding the radio waves with her distinctive voice, dominating television with her heady video, and gracing the covers of magazines like *Rolling Stone* with her wide-set, big brown eyes. Critics and fans alike couldn't help but scratch their heads with wonderment: "Who was this girl Britney Spears?" Just a short time ago she was an unknown singer from Louisiana, but now the whole world was talking about the new girl on the block whose catchy tune was stuck in everyone's head.

Like any teen on the planet, she too obsesses over pimples, bites her nails and has a tendency to hog the phone

But Britney isn't so much of a superstar that she doesn't live in the real world. She's really just like you and me. Too humble to be a diva, and too down-to-earth to take her new "it girl" status very seriously, Britney is just a normal girl who enjoys having fun like other girls her age. Like any teen on the planet, she too obsesses over pimples, bites her nails and has a tendency to hog the phone. As for Britney's weaknesses, she's got plenty, including cookie dough ice-cream, Ben Affleck movies and shopping sprees. This bubbly teen with the big voice isn't about to trade in her small town values for big time glam. Which is why she is so likeable. And as for some critics' scathing remarks that she's a one-hit wonder, a solo Spice or a Backstreet girl, this pop princess shrugs off the criticisms to pursue more important things, like her music.

Ten things you didn't know about Britney

1 Her debut hit "...Baby One More Time" was written by Max Martin, who penned many of Backstreet Boys' songs. Martin originally wrote the song for TLC, but their record company wanted Five to sing it instead. Martin then decided to give it to Britney.

2 If Britney could take three CDs with her when shipwrecked on a desert island, they would be by Lauryn Hill, Whitney Houston and Natalie Imbruglia.

3 Britney's bedroom is light blue and her shelves are filled with an impressive doll and angel collection. She also has a day-bed covered with frilly throw pillows.

4 If she could be a Spice Girl, she's said she would be Baby Spice.

5 Nothing gets her more nervous than meeting famous people – and singing in front of people she knows. But a stadium packed with thousands of fans? That's no problem for Britney.

6 The woman who plays the teacher in the video for "...Baby One More Time" is a close family friend. She's also Britney's guardian on the road. Her love interest in the video is actually Britney's cousin. He's also a model for Abercrombie & Fitch clothes.

7 Her sensible mother chose to spell Britney the way it sounds instead of sticking to the traditional spelling (Brittany). Britney's middle name is sometimes incorrectly written as Jeau in articles. It's really Jean, her grandmother's name.

8 When Britney was a kid, she kept a balance beam in the middle of her parents' living room floor for gymnastics practice. It paid off – that's really Britney doing a backflip in her video.

9 The songs "Deep In My Heart" and "I'll Never Stop Loving You" were cut from her album and replaced with the song "The Beat Goes On," originally sung by Sonny and Cher. These two songs, however, appear on the Japanese version of ...Baby One More Time.

10 When Britney needs to really chill she eats vegetable soup, listens to CDs and runs a caramel-scented bubble bath.

Britney Loves...

Superhero: Pink Power Ranger

Food: Cookie dough ice cream, pasta, hot-dogs

Drink: Sprite, mochaccino

Singers: Madonna, The Artist Formerly Known As Prince, Janet Jackson, Brandy, Natalie Imbruglia

Influences: Whitney Houston, Mariah Carey, Otis Redding

Song: "Purple Rain"

TV Show: *Dawson's Creek, Friends, Felicity*

Book: *The Horse Whisperer* by Nicholas Evans

Movies: *Titanic, My Best Friend's Wedding, Steel Magnolias, Stepmom*

Childhood Movie: *The Wizard of Oz*

Place to Live: Hawaii

Home Cooked Meal: Chicken and boiled dumplings

Actors: Brad Pitt, Ben Affleck, Tom Cruise, Joshua Jackson

Actress: Julia Roberts, Meg Ryan, Sandra Bullock

American Football Team: Atlanta Falcons

Subject: English

Gift from a Fan: a cross necklace

Basketball Player: Michael Jordan

The Essentials

Date of Birth:	December 2, 1981
Sign:	Sagittarius
Height:	5' 5"/162cm
Weight:	105 pounds/48kg
Clothes Size:	US 6
Eyes:	Brown
Hair:	Light brown
Hobbies:	Driving her go-kart, swimming, hanging out at the beach, reading Danielle Steele novels

Born To Shine

If you detected a touch of southern twang in Britney's breathy "baby, baby" in "...Baby One More Time," you're right on target. Britney Jean Spears is from the heart of America's Deep South, specifically Kentwood, Louisiana (or "Spears County" as people from her home town like to call it now), where life follows an easy, relaxed beat. Kentwood is a quiet, rural place situated an hour's drive north of swinging New Orleans. The town's population is less than 2,500, fewer people than live on one block in New York City.

Britney was born in Kentwood on December 2, 1981, about the time a girl named Madonna (now Britney's idol) was first hitting the club circuit with her own style of dance-pop. Britney's parents, Jamie and Lynne, a contractor and schoolteacher respectively, knew they had a little performer in Britney right from the start. Britney was practically singing before she could mumble 'mama.' It's as if she was born with a microphone in her hands! Her older brother Bryan can testify to that; he recalls little Brinnie skipping around the house singing Madonna's "Like a Prayer." Today her kid sister Jamie Lynne, who is ten years younger than Britney, does the same thing, only instead of singing along to Madonna, she's singing along to her older sister.

Britney was practically singing before she could mumble mama.' It's as if she was born with a microphone in her hands!

The family still lives in the cosy ranch-style house where Britney grew up. A number of trophies from Britney's talent show days adorn the bookshelves in the living room. The Spears family spends many nights gathered around the television watching sports, mostly Chicago Bulls games. Friends from around town stop by to say hello, and drop off home-baked goods like Mississippi mud pie, while laughing children ride their bikes down the tree-lined street. Although life in this small town hasn't changed much in the last few years, life for Britney has. We know her as the pop princess who draws thousands of screaming fans to her sold-out concerts; her home town has known Britney since she was just a spirited sprite trotting off to dance class.

Britney's first baby steps in ballet shoes took place at Renee Donewar's School of Dance, where she learned the difference between first position and second position, *plié* and *grande plié*, and why it takes a whole lot of practice to make a dance routine perfect. Along with rigorous dance classes, Britney enrolled in gymnastic coach Bela Karolyi's prestigious training camp, which has produced many world champion gymnasts including Nadia Comaneci. She was disciplined about attending practice and remembers crying if she missed a class. And if that wasn't enough activity in a week, she also devotedly sang gospel tunes in her church choir every Sunday. Britney was throwing herself into anything that would challenge her creativity. Before long she was taking home armfuls of trophies for her performances at talent shows and pageants; by six, the songbird-in-training had wowed the town by winning first prize at the Kentwood Dairy Festival.

Unlike her classmates, who were content playing with dolls and watching cartoons, Britney was happier perfecting a dance routine or reaching a high note.

Winning prizes at local events helped whet her appetite, but they didn't hold Britney's attention for long, she has said. By eight, Britney was bored and ready to take a bite out of something bigger. Unlike her classmates, who were content playing with dolls and watching cartoons, Britney was happier perfecting a dance routine or reaching a high note.

One day Britney's mother heard about auditions in Atlanta, Georgia for a spot on Disney's television variety show *Mickey Mouse Club*, which aired in the 1950s and was making a comeback. Before her mother could get the words 'Mickey Mouse' out of her mouth, her daughter had packed her bags and was ready to go. In fact, she begged her mother to let her audition for the coveted spot. Britney knew that it would be a crying shame if she missed an opportunity to be on a national television show. Knowing how determined her daughter was, Britney's mother consented to drive her to the Atlanta audition. Unlike the parents you often hear about who push their children to be stars so they can live out their own dreams, Britney has always said that her parents never pushed her, and never tried to make her do anything she wasn't completely willing to do on her own.

The audition went well, but the producers felt that eight-year-old Britney was too young to join the *Mickey Mouse Club*. Her efforts were not totally in vain, however. As one casting director has said, her performance was a knockout – she was truly a once-in-a-lifetime kid.

As a result of her audition, a producer from the show hooked her up with an agent in New York. Britney has said that her first trip to New York was an incredibly exciting time in her budding career. She was getting a taste of life in the big city – yellow cabs, huge crowds, posh restaurants. Who would have thought this small-town girl would end up in New York? Her town certainly didn't. In fact, many locals raised their eyebrows when they heard about Britney's bold move to the big city. 'Shouldn't she be in school?' they asked. Not when you have to follow your heart, Britney thought.

As one casting director has said, her performance was a knockout – she was truly a once-in-a-lifetime kid.

For three summers, Britney took rigorous dance classes at the Off-Broadway Dance Center and honed her skills at the Professional Performing Arts School in Manhattan. At first it was tough being a small fish in a big pond, surrounded by other kids oozing talent. But not one to crack under pressure, Britney rose above the competition. It was during this time that Britney appeared in several commercials, performed in the 1991 off-Broadway play *Ruthless*, and in 1992 nabbed a spot singing for a national audience on the television talent show *Star Search*. Britney laughs when she sees the pictures of that day. She wore a big fluffy dress and an even bigger bow in her hair. She has quipped that it looked as if she could fly away! This wonder kid was certainly keeping herself busy.

At the age of 11, Britney had an impressive array of experiences under her belt and her already noted talents had vastly improved. She was ready to audition for the *Mickey Mouse Club* again. She was among thousands of kids trying out for the coveted spot in more than a dozen cities throughout the US and Canada. This time, Britney was old enough and she successfully landed the role as a Mouseketeer! In an interview with a local newspaper at the time, she revealed that when she received the initial phone call with the news, she screamed at the top of her lungs with excitement. Her hopes for Mouseketeer status had come true. She was finally living her dream.

Britney was the youngest Mouseketeer to join the crew when she moved with her mother and kid sister to Orlando, Florida, where the show was filmed. Among her fellow Mouseketeers were Keri Russell (now the star of the popular TV show *Felicity*), and JC Chasez and Justin Timberlake (destined to be Britney's future tour mates as members of 'N Sync). She shared a dressing room with Russell and remembers vividly what life was like with JC and Justin on the set. Looking back she has said that JC was the rambunctious one, and Justin — well, he was the little guy of the group!

Her hopes for Mouseketeer status had come true. She was finally living her dream.

Together, the cast would spend two fun-filled years on the show, walking through the magical Disney World theme park together to get to the studio. Not a bad way to get to work each morning! The cast rehearsed their act all day, dancing and singing their hearts out to the show's theme song. "M-I-C see you real soon K-E-Y-Why? Because we like you-M-O-U-S-E." They even rapped to hip-hop tunes — after all, this *was* the updated *MMC*. Every week the crew had a couple of days off to do as they pleased. When Britney thinks back to those days in Orlando, she admits that her life was considerably less crazy than it is now, but it was at that time that she realized that she wanted to make a career out of music.

Sadly, in October 1994, the show was cancelled and the new friends parted ways. Britney returned home to resume a normal first year in high school. She enrolled in Park Lane Academy in nearby McComb, Mississippi, and joined the girls' basketball team. She spent a year doing what most fourteen-year-olds do, dating, shopping at the mall, and hanging out with friends. She even had braces on her teeth. But as she sat in class her thoughts started to wander. She recalls gazing out the school room window, imagining herself on a plane bound for New York, where she could continue pursuing her dreams.

The Perfect Pop Star

Britney grew more and more restless; she was desperate to stretch her wings. Whenever she had the chance she'd commute to New York from Kentwood for auditions, singing covers like "Wind Beneath My Wings." After her first taste of performing professionally on *MMC*, Britney was itching to do more of the same. She needed a big break, so her father got in touch with New York entertainment lawyer Larry Rudolph, whose clients included 98° and Ghostface Killah of Wu-Tang Clan. Rudolph asked Britney to send him photos of herself and a recording of her voice, so she got together a package right away, including a one-song demo tape of her singing over an instrumental. Rudolph, who would become her co-manager along with Johnny Wright (who also manages 'N Sync), was impressed with the young artist and knew she had a chance. Although Britney was fully aware that there are no guarantees in the music business, especially for an unknown teenager, she remained optimistic. Rudolph was also encouraging. Yes there were thousands of other artists eager to get their foot in the door, he said, but timing was everything and Britney was going for it at just the right time. Rudolph spotted a changing trend in music – the alternative grunge and gansta rap that had dominated most of the 1990s was taking a back seat, and more positive 'pop' music was making a huge comeback with bands like Backstreet Boys, Boyzone, Five and 'N Sync.

With Rudolph's help, Britney landed an audition for a new girl band called Innosense. Bizarrely, however, the manager said she was too talented and suggested she pursue a solo career instead. Rudolph then sent what Britney has called a "dinky" one-song demo tape to Jive Records, home of the Backstreet Boys. The tape landed in the hands of Jive Records' Senior Vice President of A&R (Artists and Repertoire), Jeff Fenster, who listened to the tape in amazement. Although the tape was amateur and the instrumental Britney sang over was out of her range, Fenster heard talent, so he arranged to hear Britney in person.

Britney flew into New York and went straight to Jive's offices in Manhattan. Just like any girl on the brink of getting her big break, Britney was nervous standing in front of ten bigwig executives, but she stayed focused, took a deep breath, closed her eyes and sang one of her faves, Whitney Houston's "I Have Nothing." They loved her. She was signed immediately and offered a development deal which would then lead to a solo recording contract.

The days spent gazing out of the classroom window waiting for her big break were over

At just 15, Britney had accomplished the unthinkable – scoring herself a record deal. The days spent gazing out of the classroom window waiting for her big break were over. Fenster has said that Britney possesses the rare combination of commercial appeal and the ability to convey true emotion in her singing. He knew the market was inundated with boy bands, girl bands, and boy-girl bands, and that what was desperately needed was a new young solo artist who fellow teens could relate to. He had found his girl.

Fenster introduced Britney to writer/producer Max Martin, who had worked with Backstreet Boys, Ace of Base and Robyn; he also called on writer/producer Eric Foster White, who had worked with many stars including Whitney Houston and Hi-Five. Together they would work on Britney's debut album, ...Baby One More Time.

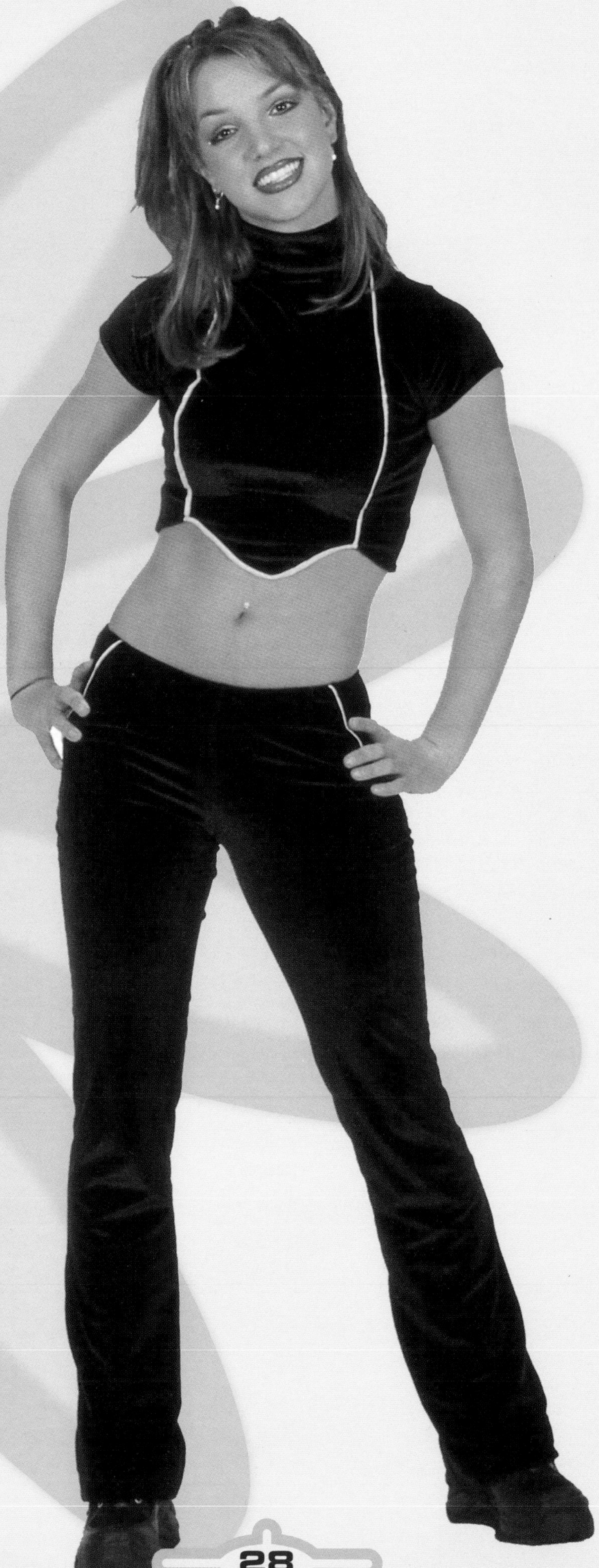

Wasting no time, Britney was bound for the Cheikron Studios in Stockholm, Sweden, where she spent most of the spring of 1998 recording songs for the album. She has said it was a joy to work with Max Martin, who is famous for his catchy melodies and infectious Eurodance rhythms, and she was thrilled to record with a talented group of musicians and vocalists.

Britney has said that she initially wanted a more adult sound similar to Natalie Imbruglia and Sheryl Crow, but after giving pure pop a try she realized it was much more her style.

Britney and Martin were originally set to work on just a couple of songs together, but because they clicked so well they ended up working on several more, including "...Baby One More Time," "I Will Be There" and "(You Drive Me) Crazy." The two worked closely on getting the album just right, and if Britney found a lyric too adult they'd change it so it was more Britney. After recording with Martin, Britney left Sweden and returned to the US, where she met with Eric Foster White to record the rest of the songs. They too collaborated closely on several songs, including "Soda Pop," "I Will Still Love You" and "E-Mail My Heart." It proved to be a busy but exciting spring for Britney.

Britney has said that she initially wanted a more adult sound similar to Natalie Imbruglia and Sheryl Crow, but after giving pure pop a try she realized it was much more her style. With funky, bass-heavy tunes like "...Baby One More Time" she could express herself in fun, synchronized dance moves. She has also made it clear that she doesn't plan on doing an Alanis Morissette by starting off with pop and then shifting gears to more alternative rock – she's happy just the way things are, and so are her fans.

After the album was complete, it was time to promote it. Britney's record company set up a website with photos of Britney, a biography and interviews with the then-unknown artist, as well as a free phone number to introduce inquisitive teens to the rising star. They also sent out hundreds of thousands of postcards announcing Britney as the girl to watch. Like 1980s pop stars Tiffany and Debbie Gibson before her, Britney embarked on a promotional tour before releasing any music. Towards the end of the summer of 1998, she toured shopping malls across the US performing a four-song set with two dancers and four wardrobe changes. She ended each performance by meeting members of the audience and handing out goody bags filled with her music and biographical information. She also met with radio DJs across the country, who found her southern grace and manners very endearing. Her tenacious spirit paid off and by October 1998, when her single "...Baby One

More Time" was first released, the response was enormous. Britney landed a coveted spot opening for 'N Sync, who were just beginning to make it big. Britney was thrilled because she was going to be reunited with her former Mouseketeers, JC Chasez and Justin Timberlake, who were no longer the little kids she remembered from *MMC*. From November to January of 1999 Britney and 'N Sync toured the US together. Opening for 'N Sync proved a great move for Britney – now she was exposing her music to an even larger audience of exuberant music fans. She was getting her first taste of tour life and she loved it! Could a girl have more fun?

But touring wasn't the only thing on Britney's mind. It was time to think video. After all, what cool song doesn't have a cool music video accompanying it? Britney knew she had to have a great video for "...Baby One More Time" – one that would fully reflect the spirit of the song. That's why she balked at an early proposal to create an animated video featuring Power Ranger-type characters. She felt the concept was too juvenile; she didn't want to appeal to four-year-olds. Britney wanted to reach people her own age, so she suggested giving the video some edge and attitude. After all, she wanted her first video to be wild!

Britney Spears

Britney was on a plane when she thought up the idea of setting it in a school. Everyone would wear school uniforms and dance and sing down the halls. Jive hired British director Nigel Dick, who had made the Backstreet Boys' video "As Long As You Love Me," to create a fun, sexy, energetic video for an equally fun, sexy, energetic song. The video was shot at Rydell High School in Venice, California, where the movie *Grease* was filmed. For two days, the crew and cast worked hard to get it just right, but between takes everyone on the set goofed around; the boys played soccer and the girls played cards and board games. Even though filming was hard work, it was a great opportunity for everyone involved to meet new friends and hang out.

The video was an immediate hit and gained heavy airplay on MTV's *Total Request Live* and Europe's The Box. Girls loved her sassy spirit in the video and boys — well, they were happy to just look at Britney. Now when she goes to press events and autograph signings Britney's flattered to hear fans rave about the video; sometime she sees girl fans sporting pink pom-poms in their hair, just like she wore in the video. Although fans loved it, some critics felt it was too sexy and criticized Britney's outfit as scandalous for a 17-year-old. Britney has defended the look, saying that all she did was don a mini-skirt and tie her boring white shirt in a knot, and that even though she bares a bit of belly, it's not as suggestive as many videos. Although every fan has a fave part in the video, Britney has said one of the best moments for her is when everyone dances in the gym at the end.

Britney's video for her second single "Sometimes" was equally as popular. Also directed by Nigel Dick, Britney sits on a beach reminiscing about a lost love. The song itself is mid-tempo, but the choreography required lots of impressive dance moves. It was while rehearsing one of these dance moves in a Los Angeles studio in February of 1999 that Britney hurt her knee. She had arrived at the studio early to go over a dance sequence and was alone in the room rehearsing one particularly difficult step where she kicks her leg high in the air. As she attempted to kick her right leg, her left leg buckled and the knee twisted to such an extent that she was sure she had broken her leg. Luckily nothing was broken, but she was forced to cancel all plans — including a European promotional tour — so she could rest. A doctor had to perform surgery to remove torn cartilage at the New Orleans Doctor's Hospital, and Britney had to spend at least four weeks recovering.

At a time when she should have been jumping for joy at her album's success, Britney was limited to her couch at home

For a while she was confined to a wheelchair, and later had to totter about on crutches. This wasn't always easy for Britney, who was determined to complete her video for "Sometimes." In the middle of it all, she was chosen to appear in *People* magazine's highly regarded "Fifty Most Beautiful People" issue. A photo shoot was required, so a hobbling Britney endured hours of flashing bulbs to get the picture just right. What a trooper! She also forfeited the chance to present an award at the Forty-First Annual Grammy Awards in February. Even though she wouldn't be partying with her fellow recording artists, Britney did present the award via satellite.

She has said that the mishap was a blessing in disguise and that her body needed the rest

At a time when she should have been jumping for joy at her album's success, Britney was limited to her couch at home. Her leg hurt and she was annoyed about missing her European tour, but she has said that the mishap was a blessing in disguise and that her body needed the rest. After all, she had been working non-stop for a year recording her CD, making a video and touring with 'N Sync.

Amazing Statistics

1 Britney's album ...*Baby One More Time* reached Platinum status in the US, Canada and England, selling more than one million copies in each country.

2 In the UK the single "...Baby One More Time" picked up the fourth-highest sales in one week ever, beaten only by Band Aid's "Do They Know It's Christmas", Wham's "Last Christmas" and Elton John's "Candle In The Wind '97."

3 Her America Online Internet chat was the fourth most popular individual chat in AOL's history.

4 Britney is the youngest person ever to have sold more than a million copies of a debut single in the UK.

5 She's the first female artist (and the youngest) to simultaneously have the number one single on the Billboard 100 and the number one album on the Billboard 200 charts. Her album looks set to be the biggest seller of 1999 by far.

6 Britney's number one album broke records by climbing the US charts higher and higher each week for five weeks.

7 Her video for "...Baby One More Time" was one of the most requested ever on MTV's *Total Request Live.*

8 "...Baby One More Time" was the first record to spend more than a week at number one in the UK for eleven weeks, and the record company had to press extra copies to meet the overwhelming demand.

9 The album sold 124,000 copies in the UK on the first day of release alone, 1000 more than Lenny Kravitz, the previous number one, had sold in six days.

10 "...Baby One More Time" has been number one in the US, Canada, the UK and New Zealand, and number two in Holland, Sweden, Norway and Australia.

Britney and Boys

Boys, boys, boys. What question does Britney get asked most often? "Does she have a boyfriend?" After all, most of her songs are about love, so she must have a string of boyfriends. Well the truth is, right now she doesn't have any. Britney certainly has her crushes like any girl, but she has said it's almost impossible to have a relationship when you spend most of your time flying from one country to the next.

Although she certainly has her pick of eligible guys who would love to go out on a date with her, her hectic schedule — touring, interviews, promotional events and working on future projects — doesn't leave her with much time to even think about boys. But that doesn't mean boys around the world aren't interested. When Britney finished recording a segment for MTV's *Total Request Live*, she walked out of the building in New York's Times Square to a crowd of adoring guys who had the words "Will You Go to the Prom With Me?" scrawled on their chests. When she visited a record store in London, an army of guys waited outside just to get a glimpse of her. And if you surf the web, you'll find endless fan web sites dedicated to her.

She has said it's almost impossible to have a relationship when you spend most of your time flying from one country to the next.

Britney admits she has been in love — with Reg, her high school sweetheart, who she dated for two years in Louisiana — but the demands of her career took their toll on the relationship and the two lovebirds went their separate ways. She has said that it's difficult to maintain a long distance relationship — she hates having to rely on phone conversations — which is the only kind of relationship she can really have on the road.

As for the second most-commonly-asked question — what was her first kiss like? — well, she's said it was pretty forgettable. When Britney was interviewed by a fan on MTV's *FANatic*, a show that lets a devoted fan interview an all-time fave artist, Britney confessed that her first kiss was OK, but the next day the boy totally ignored her, leaving Britney rather hurt.

Although she doesn't have a boyfriend now, she keeps her eyes open. She's smitten for Ben Affleck and would love to go out to dinner with Brad Pitt, who happens to be a Sagittarius just like Britney. On the topic of more attainable boys, she likes a loving lad with a wonderful personality. Sure he has to be good looking, but Britney isn't going to be bothered with a boy who's got a pretty face but nothing to say. She says a boy with a happy outlook on life is key and that he should have a healthy dose of self-confidence. She'll admit that a guy is especially swoon-worthy if he's got a good sense of fun – this girl likes a good laugh.

Although she doesn't have a boyfriend now, she keeps her eyes open.

For the guys taking note, there's more. Like any girl-guy dynamic, it's always more intriguing if there's a dose of mystery in the relationship, which is why Britney likes a boy to play hard to get. She doesn't want to play games, but she certainly doesn't want someone to come on too strong either. This Sagittarius loves her freedom, so the more you let her breathe, the more intrigued she'll be.

She'll admit that a guy is especially swoon-worthy if he's got a good sense of fun – this girl likes a good laugh.

As for relationship woes, well, Britney has her opinions. She has said that if another girl started flirting with her other half she'd try to stay calm and keep her feelings to herself. If the guy took the bait and went with the other girl – well, he's history and he wasn't meant to be anyway.

Although her hectic schedule means Britney doesn't get to do much dating, she has offered her own words of advice: First, be yourself – you want someone to like you for you, not someone you're trying to be. Second, don't worry too much about what you're wearing or what he's thinking; none of that matters when you've got chemistry working for you. Third, have fun and if the date went well and you like the guy, well, make sure you get a kiss in by the end of the night!

Then there's the issue of music. Britney has said that she loves slow-dancing cheek-to-cheek to beautiful love songs like Eric Clapton's "Wonderful Tonight." But when she wants to do some serious dancing she likes fast tunes from Mariah Carey or Matchbox 20. For serious grooving, she'll choose Van Morrison's "Brown Eyed Girl" — after all, she is one.

Like everyone else her age, she's still trying to figure out relationships and boys. The key to knowing how Britney feels is to listen to her songs. In "Sometimes" she sings about a shy girl trying to approach a crush, and in "E-mail My Heart" ("All I do is check the screen to see if you're okay") she offers a new take on love in the 1990s. She has said that e-mails are like modern versions of the old-fashioned love letter, only better.

Britney has said that she loves slow-dancing cheek-to-cheek to beautiful love songs like Eric Clapton's "Wonderful Tonight."

Hanging With Her Girlfriends

What would life be like without your best mates to share stuff with? For Britney, friendship is super important. She made friends with all sorts of people when she was at Park Lane Academy high school. She has said that the school was full of cliques just like in the movie *Clueless*, but she broke boundaries and made friends with everyone. Britney tries to stay in touch with her friends as much as she can when she's far from Kentwood. On the road, she relies on e-mail to catch up with her pals and to gossip about boys. She's a great believer in the Internet as a brilliant way to stay connected – and it's a lot cheaper than phone calls.

Having been brought up to keep long distance phone calls to a minimum, Britney is careful not to run up high phone bills – although she's started to use a cellular phone now that she's touring so much, which hasn't helped. When Britney is home in Kentwood, which she tries to arrange at least every four weeks, she likes to do girl stuff with her friends like shopping, throwing slumber parties, getting her hair done and watching movies. She has said that because she comes from a close-knit town, everybody knows everybody, so her close friends are like sisters.

In a friend, Britney has said that she looks for someone she can really trust and who is really honest – someone who will tell you the truth even if you don't want to hear it. Because friendship is so important to her, Britney has made an effort to make sure her old friends still view her the same way as they always did. When she's back in the US, Britney also hangs out with Danielle Fishel, the star of the popular television show *Boy Meets World*.

She has said that school was full of cliques just like in the movie *Clueless*, but she broke boundaries and made friends with everyone.

One of her best friends is her mother, who Britney has said she admires for her relentless positivity. Although she's close to her dad, who she has said is very affectionate and treats her like his baby girl, it's her mother who she most resembles. This means she's got her mother's weaknesses, like biting her nails and worrying about every little thing she has said. Just as with her girlfriends, Britney can count on her mother to always be there, and often calls her when she's on the road for advice. After the success of her album, Britney treated her mother to a diamond-laden tennis bracelet as a thankyou gift.

One of her best friends is her mother, who Britney has said she admires for her relentless positivity.

So is Britney planning on flying around the world with her friends to celebrate the millennium? Hardly. Her mother has said that Britney is staying put in Kentwood for the millennium, because she's worried about the 'millennium bug' and wants her daughter safe at home in Kentwood. So while some pop stars party in Times Square, New York, Britney plans to usher in the year 2000 with family and friends at home.

She's Got The Look

No one likes dressing up more than Britney. She loves flicking through magazines like *Cosmopolitan* to check out the latest trends, and has a passion for new outfits and cool shoes. She has said that Jennifer Aniston and Jennifer Love Hewitt are her fashion icons, and loves waiting to see what they'll wear next. When it's time to get dolled up for awards shows or a night out on the town, Britney likes to shop at BeBe. To present an award at the American Music Awards in January in Los Angeles, she wore a gorgeous white satin sheath dress and a sparkling tiara. The glamorous get-up won rave reviews in the gossip columns.

She also loves Betsey Johnson's stunning dresses, the classy look of Giorgio Armani, chic Donna Karan outfits and Calvin Klein's ever-creative designs. When she's on the road this "Tommy Girl" likes to wear comfy clothes from Tommy Hilfiger, and loves casual khakis and shirts from Abercrombie & Fitch. When she's home, she admits to wearing the essential comfort clothes — sweat pants and a T-shirt.

When she's on the road this "Tommy Girl" likes to wear comfy clothes from Tommy Hilfiger

As for accessories to jazz up an outfit, Britney keeps it simple. She often wears one of her fave accessories, diamond stud earrings, but generally she thinks a clean, classic look is best achieved by keeping extras to a minimum.

Even though her schedule is crazy, Britney does make time for a little shopping in each city she visits, and has said she especially likes the fashions in London. A self-confessed shopaholic, Britney is always keeping her eye out for cute new outfits and likes to collect hats – she has over 20 already. Because Britney loves light blue, you'll often see her wearing it both on and off the stage. For the World Music Awards in Monte Carlo in May of 1999, Britney wore a stunning midnight blue velvet top with a matching skirt that sparkled. She has a stylist who makes her concert clothes – Britney thinks up a look and the stylist works her magic.

But what about Britney's beauty tips? How does 17-year-old Britney keep her complexion clean when she's up against the same skin problems as any teenager? Her secret to fighting off the spots is to drink lots of water, eat well and get as much sleep as possible. She also maintains a radiant glow by working out, which keeps her blood pumping and her body healthy. In order to perfect her intensive dance routines during her concerts, Britney exercises as much as she can with squats, calf lifts and stomach crunches, so when it's time to perform on stage her dance routines are flawless.

A self–confessed shopaholic, Britney is always keeping her eye out for cute new outfits.

When it comes to make-up, Britney has started to experiment with the latest style – shimmery pastels. It was during a magazine makeover that Britney discovered the subtle, pick-me-up qualities of peach. A make-up artist replaced her dark eyeliner with a touch of mascara on her lashes and applied a soft peach eyeshadow below her brow bone to accent her eyes. He also replaced her muted matte lipstick with a subtle pale lip gloss for an ethereal look. For her hair, a stylist used extensions to lengthen her blonde highlighted locks. She's taken to wearing the hair extensions for performances, and also likes sporting pigtails like in the video for "…Baby One More Time." When she's at a big event, she crimps her hair for a more dressy look. Eyeshadow, lipstick and hair extensions are added beauty bonuses, but her most reliable routine is simply to flash a big broad smile.

Britney On The Road

Britney has said that one of the best things about being a pop star is making new friends around the world. At the end of summer 1998, after she had finished recording her album, Britney got her first taste of life on the road when she kicked off an intensive promotional tour. Along with two male backing singers and four wardrobe changes, Britney trekked across the US performing a four-song routine at shopping malls. This was before her single had even been released to the public, and way before she was even a blip on the radio radar. For the first time, she was singing to a crowd of kids who didn't know who she was. She said that it was nerve-wracking at first, but she went for it. It was a great chance to meet her fellow teens and introduce her music. The positive response was tremendous.

Her second big public performance was in November 1998, when she landed the coveted opening spot on 'N Sync's US tour. Although she admits it was difficult performing in front of hordes of girls screaming for 'N Sync, Britney managed to win them over by her second song. Soon thousands of girls in packed stadiums across the US were screaming her name.

It was just after she had finished her tour with 'N Sync that her album made its US chart debut. It would catapult to the number one slot a week later.

Although it sounds like every girl's dream to tour with the hot guys from 'N Sync, the two acts were way too busy to spend much time hanging out, and only briefly saw each other at lunch and dinner. Britney has said that she was nervous when she first joined the tour with 'N Sync, because she had assumed they'd be too cool for her. But when she was reunited with former Mouseketeers JC Chasez and Justin Timberlake she says they were the same sweet, funny guys she remembered from *MMC*. It was just after she had finished her tour with 'N Sync that her album made its US chart debut. It would catapult to the number one slot a week later.

Britney made a brief promotional visit to England at the beginning of February 1999, but she had to cancel all her promotional engagements when she injured her knee. Although she wasn't in the UK for long, she remembers her gruelling schedule. She recalls waking up early and appearing on TV show after TV show, doing interview after interview, gobbling a quick bite to eat in the tour bus and fixing her hair before continuing with the next interview.

Britney wowed the audience yet again with her performance – and her long black wig!

She returned to Europe in May 1999 when she performed at the World Music Awards in Monte Carlo. Britney wowed the audience yet again with her performance – and her long black wig! When she returned to the US that same month, Britney made a special performance at a junior high school in Savannah, Georgia as part of TV channel Nickelodeon's "Nick Takes Over Your School Sweepstakes." The schoolkids were thrilled to take a break from the books to hear Britney perform live in their school. Britney has also

made a spectacular impression on a number of popular talk shows in 1999, including *The Rosie O'Donnell Show* and *The Tonight Show With Jay Leno*.

As this book is being written, Britney is in the middle of her first headlining tour of the US and Canada, visiting 50 cities! The tour began in Florida at the end of June, and continues right through the summer up until early September. After touring North America, Britney is packing her bags and embarking on a European tour. She has said that she is looking forward to the different clothes, cultures and foods she encountered last time she was in Europe. She found London particularly cool, and remarked that the people were "awesome."

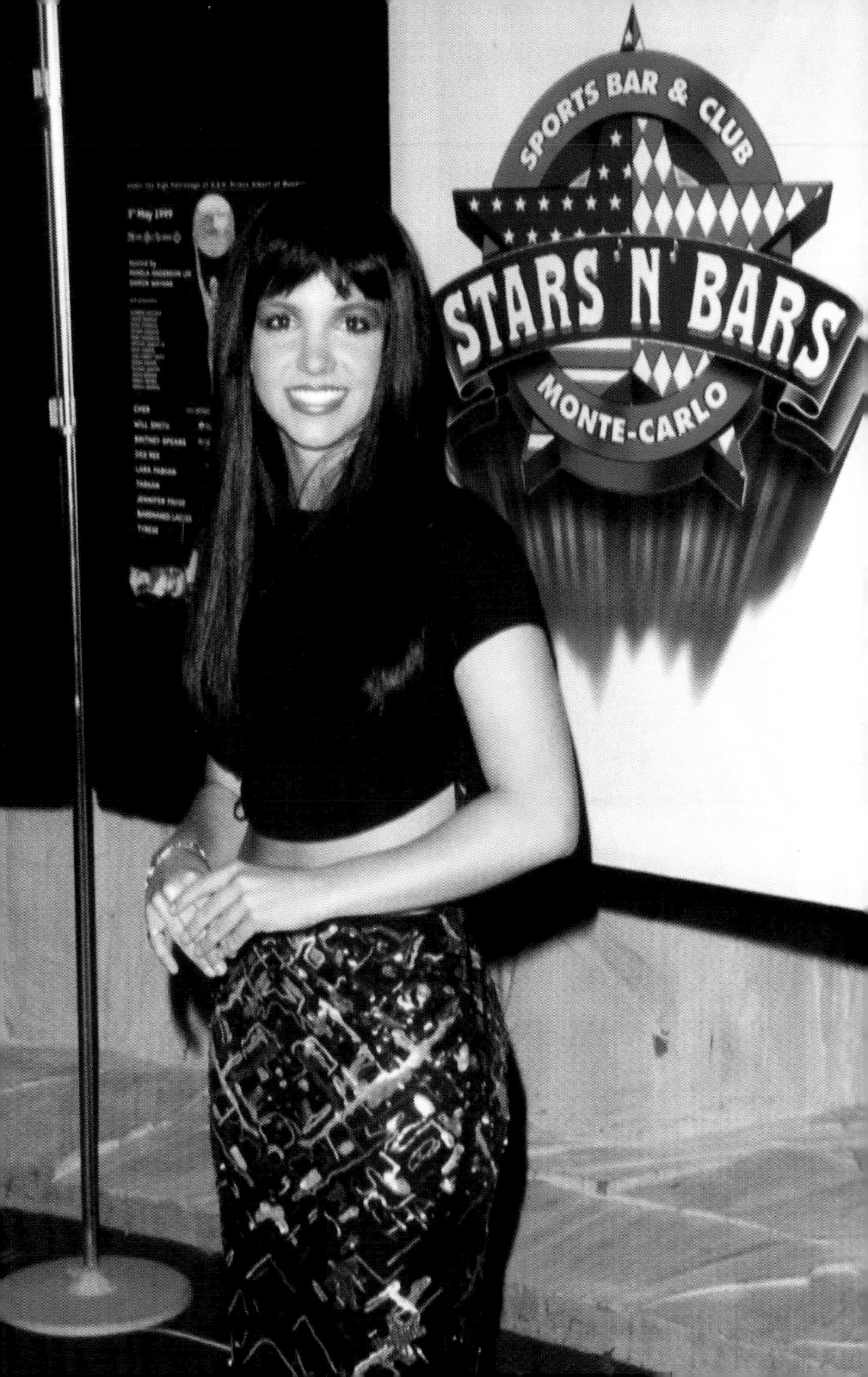
SPORTS BAR & CLUB
STARS 'N' BARS
MONTE-CARLO

Naturally, as with any live performance, there are no guarantees that everything will go as planned. Britney remembers one performance when she was dancing across the stage and her foot slipped on a cupcake that someone had thrown on the stage! She took a nasty spill and landed heavily. Luckily all was forgotten when her dancers helped her up and Britney, being the professional that she is, continued with the performance. She's also lost her headset during a song. Another time she disguised a pimple on her face with eyeliner so it would look like a mole. Unfortunately, the "mole" ended up looking a big mess after her sweaty routine smeared the make-up all over her face! There are bound to be many more mishaps down the road, but fortunately experience has taught Britney to get on with the show, even if she is a little red in the face with embarrassment!

Although her pop star schedule on the road means much sleep deprivation, she tries to get in ten hours of sleep a night if she can. She admits that she doesn't bother looking at her long list of things to do anymore. Instead she takes things one day at a time. Although this Southern Baptist girl tries to attend church every Sunday, it's not always possible while she's on tour, so she prays nightly.

Because her mother thought it was best to stay at home in Kentwood with her sister Jamie Lynne, who is ten years younger than Britney, Britney travels on the road with a close family friend, who makes sure Britney has time for studying. She is currently doing a correspondence course with the University of Nebraska, and has said that English is her fave subject because she loves to read. As for Trigonometry and Spanish – she's not so keen on these!

The Beat Goes On

Fans are shouting "Hit it Britney, we want more," and the good news is she's going to deliver just that. Not only is she touring the US, and soon Europe, but Britney is starting to write more of her own songs. These include "I'm So Curious," which is featured on the B-side of her second single "Sometimes."

Like Backstreet Boys, Jennifer Love Hewitt and Joshua Jackson before her, Britney will sport a frothy white moustache in a "Got Milk?" ad, part of one of the highest profile campaigns in US advertising history. She'll also make a guest appearance in October on the Disney Channel show *The Famous Jett Jackson* and she's planning to star in a McDonald's commercial along with sports star Sammy Sosa.

In May Britney launched her official web site (http://www.britney.com) in response to the overwhelming demand for more Britney online. The new official web site features never-before-seen photographs, travel diaries, fashion stuff and Britney's international news. Portions of the site are available in Japanese and other languages. Speaking of Japan, some remarkably cute Britney dolls are on sale there right now, dressed just like Britney in the video for "...Baby One More Time." Look out for more Britney merchandise on sale around the world in the coming months.

In May Britney launched her official web site (http://www.britney.com)

Britney is also currently negotiating with Columbia TriStar to appear in at least three upcoming episodes of her fave television show, *Dawson's Creek*. There are also plans to create a drama or comedy for Britney for the year 2000, in which she's said she'll play someone "not too serious!" Like R&B artist Brandy, who has combined a successful music career with a starring role in the television show *Moesha*, Britney is destined to cross over into television and perhaps movies after that. She has promised her fans that she will never abandon music and will continue to make records — she already has plans to work on a new album in 2000. This ambitious girl is always looking to the future.

Britney has said that in the next two or three years she would like to produce tracks, and if time allows she wants to learn the guitar. "My career goals are basically to continue to do what I'm doing now and just get better and grow as an artist and be a legend like Madonna or Janet Jackson. That would be cool," she said during a live Internet chat.

In the mid-1980s, when Britney was just starting to dance and sing around the house, a rising star named Madonna told Dick Clark on the TV talent show *American Bandstand* that she wanted to conquer the world. At the time people rolled their eyes, but after a few years and several major hits Madonna would live up to those very words. More than a decade later, a rising star named Britney Spears echoed those same words when she told a reporter, "I want to conquer the world." Will Britney achieve her goal? Time will tell, like it always does.

Many fans are wondering if there will be a Grammy waiting for Britney at the Forty-Second Annual Grammy Awards in 2000. We'll keep our fingers crossed Britney!

"My career goals are basically to continue to do what I'm doing now and just get better and grow as an artist and be a legend like Madonna or Janet Jackson. That would be cool."

Test Your Britney Trivia

Now that you've read all about Britney Spears, you and a friend can test your Britney IQ with this quiz. Good luck!

1. Britney has said she'd love to go out to dinner with:
a. Robbie Williams
b. Nick Carter
c. Brad Pitt

2. How old was Britney when she joined the cast of the *Mickey Mouse Club*?
a. 8
b. 11
c. 17

3. Britney has the habit of:
a. singing in the bathtub
b. worrying too much
c. biting her nails

4. What is Britney planning on doing for the millennium?
a. singing in Times Square, New York
b. shopping in London
c. staying at home in Kentwood

5. Which 1960s artist has Britney said influenced her?
a. John Lennon
b. Elvis Presley
c: Otis Redding

6. Britney's top subject in school is:

a. English

b. Geometry

c. Biology

7. Which European country does Britney love for its style?

a. France

b. England

c. Holland

8. When did Britney realize she wanted music to be her career?

a. after the *Mickey Mouse Club*

b. after starring in the off-Broadway play *Ruthless*

c. after listening to Michael Jackson's album *Thriller* when she was a kid

9. What gets Britney really nervous?

a. singing to a packed stadium

b. meeting famous people

c. dancing on stage

10. Britney's secret of success is ...

a. express yourself and remember that you have a talent, so use it

b. work hard and never give up

c. Be positive and go for your dreams

1 – c, 2 – b, 3 – all of them!, 4 – c, 5 – c, 6 – c, 7 – b, 8 – a, 9 – b, 10 – all of them!

Answers

Discography

Singles

"...Baby One More Time"
Jive, Released November 1998

"...Baby One More Time"
BMG International, Released February 1999
Highest Chart Position: 1

"Sometimes"
Jive, Released April 1999
Highest Chart Position: 27

"Sometimes"
BMG International, Released June 1999
Highest Chart Position: 3

Albums

"...Baby One More Time"
Jive, Released January 1999
Highest Chart Position: 1

"...Baby One More Time"
BMG International, Released February 1999
Highest Phart Position: 1
...Baby One More Time/ (You Drive Me) Crazy/Sometimes/Soda Pop/Born To
Make You Happy/From the Bottom of My Broken Heart/I Will Be There/ I
Will Still Love You/Thinkin' About You/E-mail My Heart/The Beat Goes On

Compilations

Sabrina, The Teenage Witch Soundtrack
(Various Artists)
Geffen, October 1998
Walk of Life – Spice Girls/Abracadabra – Sugar Ray/Hey Mr. DJ (Keep Playin'
This Song – Backstreet Boys)/One Way Or Another – Melissa Joan Hart/Kate – Ben
Folds Five/Show Me Love (Radio Edit) – Robyn/Giddy Up – N Sync/Slam Dunk
(Da Funk) – Five/Magnet & Steel – Matthew Sweet/ So I Fall Again – Phantom
Planet/I Know What Boys Like – Pure Sugar/Smash – The Murmurs, Jane
Wiedlin, Charlotte Caffey/Doctor Jones (Metro 7lm Edit) – Aqua/Soda
Pop – Britney Spears/Amnesia (Radio Remix) – Chumbawamba/Blah, Blah,
Blah – The Cardigans